Two Decades of Scottish Steam

Strathwood

Two Decades of Scottish Steam

Donald Peddie

Strathwood

Two Decades of Scottish Steam

My engine now is cold and still,
No water does my boiler fill;
My coke affords its flame no more
My days of usefulness are o'er.

My wheels deny their noted speed
No more my guiding hand they need.
My whistle, too has lost its tone
Its shrill and thrilling sound are gone.

My valves are now thrown open wide
My flanges all refuse to guide.
My cranks also, once so strong.
Refuse to aid the busy throng.
No more I feel each urging breath,
My steam is now condensed in death.

Life's railways o'er, each station's passed,
In death I'm stopped and rest at last.
Farewell dear friends and cease to weep,
In Christ I'm safe, in Him I Sleep.

Active with steam to the last Ian Peddie on the footplate of the oldest surviving Black Five on the Strathspey Railway in the late 1980s.

First published 2008

ISBN 1-905276-07-9   ISBN 978-1-905276-07-3

Copyright Strathwood Ltd 2008 Published by Strathwood Ltd

Contents

Foreword

My father, Ian Peddie, who died in 2006, photographed the Scottish railway scene in the final two decades of steam locomotive operation. In choosing a selection of his photographs for this publication I have two objectives in mind: firstly, to provide a fitting tribute to him and his photographic work and secondly, to allow fellow enthusiasts a glimpse of a bygone age, in which many items of pre-grouping rolling stock were still in everyday use. Additionally, since my father took notes for all his photographs, the sharing of this material and related anecdotes provides a further explicit memorial.

His interest in Scottish railway photography started in the late 1940s. He was mainly interested in recording pre-grouping locomotives and rolling stock and capturing what was, in the early 1950s, a disappearing scene.

Living in Stirling he naturally focused this record on Stirling and the Scottish central belt, and whilst visits were made to other railway centres, it was never the case that photographs were a "must" to record each visit. Moreover, since he had little interest in post-grouping locomotives, several LMS and LNER designed locomotives, such as 4P Compounds and K2 Moguls, were not recorded.

As an engineer, my father was at home in a locomotive works or running shed. As a result, the majority of his work excludes station scenes. Armed with his British Railways Scottish Region photographic pass - which he held from 1951 to 1969 - he could plan his shed visits without the need to request individual permits. Additionally, his hobby was greatly assisted through his marriage to a railwayman's daughter, who accompanied many visits with supportive forbearance.

Whilst not a railway employee, he had a great many friends who were. At Stirling, if unusual locomotives appeared on the shed, he would be called at home: hence he recorded 54398, Ben Alder, at Stirling, in November 1958, on her way to hoped-for preservation. Only latterly did he take any real interest in more modern locomotives. He was much more interested in say a Highland Railway brake van or a North British, gas-lit, 3rd class coach, than in powerful, modern locomotives.

In his Scottish railway travels he acquired photographs of older pre-grouping locomotives and a few of these have been included purely from a nostalgic viewpoint. His interest in railways along with myself accompanying him on trips from an early age, as illustrated in both of these photographs, fostered my own lifetime hobby.

I am grateful to the publishers, Strathwood Books, for their support with this project. Any errors in photographic captions, can be laid squarely on the content of my father's notebooks, for which I take full responsibility.

16366 at Stirling South 6th March 1949

55126 at Stirling South September 1950

I recently recalled in the preparation of this book that one or two of my father's railway friends had attended his funeral in 2006 and I have managed to make contact with two of them. The two are George Tainsh, who started his railway career at the Stirling LNER shed in 1946 and Robert Eggo, who was attached to the Stirling LMS shed, having started work there in 1938. I found that in late 2007 these two long standing engine drivers at Stirling, were able to add a wealth of information to these two fabulous photographs in my father's collection that serve to illustrate how things were around the time when he was born and in his earlier years. Its quite amazing how elderly folks can recall details from fifty plus years ago.

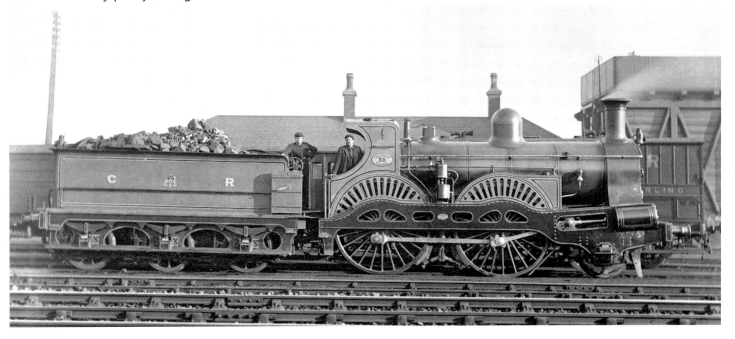

Caledonian Railway No 30

Built by Neilson & Co in 1872 to a Benjamin Connor design, and rebuilt with Drummond boiler at St. Rollox in 1899. Transferred to duplicate list as No.1030 in 1912 and withdrawn from traffic in 1917 when my father was four years old. Photographed at Burghmuir (the location of the Caledonian Railway sheds at Stirling) in 1908. The driver is John Todd, whose son Peter Todd was also a Stirling driver, the latter becoming a running foreman at Stirling shed in LMS days. The fireman is Ebenezar Kirkpatrick, whose descendants live in Stirling.

Caledonian Railway No 59

Built at St Rollox in 1902 to a J.F. McIntosh design for the Oban line traffic, and withdrawn from service in 1936 as LMS No 14604. This superb photograph from the pre-grouping period was also taken at Burghmuir this time in 1906. In charge of the engine on this day was Driver A. Snedden.

Alexander Ian Peddie (7th July 1913 - 22nd September 2006)

It is my privilege to pay a tribute to my father Alexander Ian Peddie, whom we all loved in our own special and particular ways, and who will be remembered for many years, with gratitude and for the influence he had on our respective lives.

Ian, as he was always known, was essentially the combination of a family man, a North Church man and a Stirling man.

He was born at 33 Abbey Road, Stirling on the 7th of July 1913 and baptised by the Revd. D. P. McLees in the old North Church in Murray Place on the 5th August in that year. Ian's parents were North Church members, who came from Perth.

The family moved to Stirling in 1912, when his father became the commercial clerk at the Graham & Morton furniture factory, which was then located in Colquhoun Street, Stirling, just a stone's throw from the church where this eulogy was read on the 27th September 2006.

Through army war service in India, his father died when young Ian was six, his father's sacrifice being commemorated on the North Church War Memorial now installed at this same church.

Early schooling at the Allan's School, Spittal Street, Stirling, was followed by transfer to The High School of Stirling. Aged ten he won a bursary to support his attendance and from there he started an apprenticeship with the then Harland Engineering Company at Alloa, in August 1928.

Very surprisingly, he remained employed by Harland and their successors at Alloa, until his retirement from a senior position in 1978, aged sixty five, having completed an uninterrupted working span of fifty years with one employer. My father had absolutely no regrets about this.

He recalled that life was tough in the 1920s/1930s - his starting wage was 6/10d per week - the equivalent of around 35 pence today - and his mother lost the 10/s per week war widow's allowance for him when he started work. On the plus side, however, his mother and her two sisters ran a dressmaking & furriers business in Stirling and this kept the family in continuing modest prosperity.

Despite various offers of employment elsewhere (for example, Chief Electrical Engineer of a Chilean copper smelter high in the Andes, or Deputy Superintendent of Glasgow Corporation Tramways power system - where he spent much time installing Harland plant in the 1930s - or as Manager of the Harland factory at Timperley, in Manchester, to name but three), he chose to remain in Stirling, the town he loved.

He was well travelled in business, and celebrated the birth of his first grand-daughter in 1972, whilst dealing with company technical problems at Muffeleera, in the Zambian copper belt.

It would be no exaggeration to say that he loved his work, and happily in retirement he continued to provide sound technical advice and wise counsel on various interesting projects to his former employers.

Amongst his papers, I have come across the results of the Army, Hostilities Only, Commissioning Board dated 1940; from the related letter it is clear that he was to be commissioned into The Royal Engineers. However, he was diverted into the management of the production and inspection of sub-assemblies for Lancaster bombers and Sunderland flying boat for the then Ministry of Aircraft Production.

In parallel with this war work, he volunteered for duty in the Auxiliary Fire Service in Stirling and served for four years as a company officer.

In 1944, he married my mother Mary Roxburgh, from Hurlford, Ayrshire, and they had over fifty years of happy married life until her passing away in 1999.

In addition to his work, his real hobby was railway photography and all matters connected with Scottish railways: many of his Saturdays were spent visiting railway facilities across Scotland, where he had many friends. As you might imagine, this hobby required a degree of forbearance from my mother, since quite often, annual holidays seemed selected to give the opportunity for father to visit local railways. Many holidays were focused on narrow gauge railways in Wales - they were, I can assure you great holidays.

It would be unthinkable at this time not to mention father's driving record. Like his peers, he sat no test of any type, yet was licensed to drive all manner of road vehicles including tramcars, fire engines, steam traction engines and so forth. He started driving in 1929 and very reluctantly gave up his licence aged ninety two, in 2004. With great pride, he maintained he had an unblemished, clean licence for seventy three years, which was only partially true. He got very cross if reminded of his 1940 conviction and £2 fine for running into the back of a steam traction engine on the Alloa road in the blackout. His license was not endorsed as the magistrate believed father's evidence that the traction engine driver had lit his red tail lamp after the accident!

Father had a fund of early motoring stories, one concerning the first set of traffic lights installed in Stirling in 1930, at the junction of Wallace Street and Cowan Street. They were very much a novelty and motorists of the day initially found them hard to deal with. On one occasion father had stopped rather quickly as the lights changed and was run into quite severely by the car behind. The offending driver got out, expressed profuse apologies and quite innocently asked father if he could borrow a spanner to tighten up his brakes.

Ian Peddie was ordained an elder in the North Church in 1963 and served in that capacity actively for more than twenty years, only giving up regular attendance at morning worship due to my mother's increasing infirmity.

Throughout his life, my father was surrounded by women. In his youth, he was brought up by his mother, her two sisters, and two maiden aunts from his father's family. There is no doubt he was thoroughly spoiled at this time and this continued in his latter years through the loving attentions of his five grand-daughters.

Always an intensely private individual, he was a man of principle, honour and integrity in all he undertook, whether at home, at work or wherever.

He was much loved by his wife, his two children, his five grandchildren and his three great grandchildren. He will be greatly missed.

A photographic opportunity not to be missed was on the 10th April 1950 when 14409 Ben Alisky one of the Highland Railway 2P "Small Ben" locomotives was caught at Stirling South in steam on her way to Kilmarnock Works for scrapping.

This was another of my late father's favourites. D30 4-4-0 62427 Dumbiedykes seen here at Stirling Shore Road in February 1957. His notes indicated that he travelled upon it between Stirling and Alloa in 1953.

Stirling - Shore Road (from 1949, Stirling North)

The main LNER engine shed at Stirling, known as Shore Road, was located adjacent to Forth Street in the Riverside area, the entrance being via the LNER goods yard entry off Forth Place. The shed, a two road building, was built in the 1850s for the Stirling & Dunfermline Railway, which was absorbed by the North British Railway.

Geographically, the depot was located to the north of Stirling station and on the east side of the LNER main line to Alloa: the depot could be seen from the north end of Platform 1 at Stirling station.

Additionally, and opposite Shore Road shed, but on the west side of the LMS main line to Perth, the LNER had workshops where locomotive repairs were carried out into the late 1930s and where wagon and carriage repairs continued until the early 1950s. These works, known as Cowpark Works, had been the workshops of the Forth & Clyde Railway, and lay in a triangle bounded on the north by Lover's Walk, on the east by the LMS main line to Perth and in the west by the LNER branch line to Gargunnock, Kippen and beyond. The entrance to Cowpark Works was at the bottom of Wallace Street, opposite Provost Bain's clock. The Cowpark works site is now occupied by the Stirling ambulance depot.

Shore Road was an interesting shed to visit, since in the late 1940s many former NBR named locomotives appeared there on services from Glasgow (Queen Street), and Edinburgh (Waverley). Additionally, local services to Perth via the Devon Valley line plus other local passenger and goods traffic ensured a variety of motive power. There was a daily shunt of rolling stock for repair between Shore Road goods yard and Cowpark Works and even in the early 1950s the enginemen on this duty referred to the working as "crossing the blue line" since the former Caledonian Railway main line to Perth bisected the two LNER sites - loyalties die hard in railway circles.

Shore Road depot closed in 1957, at which time the shed and adjacent goods sidings had become very overgrown and neglected. In its final months, Shore Road hosted many locomotives from the former LMS shed at Burghmuir (known latterly as Stirling South), whilst the latter was being re-equipped with new workshops and turntable.

General view of the former NBR shed at Shore Road on the 8th September 1956, with ex NBR Class J37s 64585, 64542 and 64595 visible.

These two views of ex NBR Class J35 64501 were recorded at Shore Road on the 20th January 1951 and on the 30th April 1949. In the former, 64501 is on the Shore Road turntable post Westinghouse brake removal. The latter shows the engine as previously fitted with Westinghouse brake along with the LNER modified 6 in the cab numbering.

The setting sun captures ex NBR Class D34 2489, Glen Dessary at Shore Road on the 2nd November 1948. Allocated to Eastfield, 2489 had worked a Glasgow, Queen Street to Stirling passenger train. This engine was not renumbered as 62489 until February 1950 which she held until withdrawn in 1959.

The 2nd of November 1948 also found another ex NBR design with a Class J88 68346 shunting the Shore Road goods yard. In latter LNER days two J88s were based at Stirling, one loco being stationed at Alloa for shunting the harbour branch. As can be seen the J88's water tank has been subject to "make do and mend" riveting repairs and the painting has not fully eliminated the initial LNER number 9132. The smokebox numberplate has the correct Gill Sans style for 6, whereas the bunker number is painted with the LNER modified 6.

In 1955 Pickersgill designed ex CR 3P 54504 was transferred from Hurlford to Shore Road to support passenger traffic, and was recorded there now settled in on the 14th April 1956. In April 1959 she would go into store at Forfar until officially withdrawn that December.

Still dressed in her LNER livery was ex NBR Class D33 2460 at Shore Road on the 28th August 1948. An Eastfield engine, 2460 had worked a passenger train from Glasgow, Queen Street, to Stirling, via Greenhill and would return to Glasow on an opposite working. The locomotive was withdrawn from Eastfield shed in August 1951.

On the 16th August 1952, "Dunalastair IV" 54447, a Perth engine, was at Shore Road shed and retains its original two piece chimney. Perth engines worked passenger traffic to Stirling via the LNER Devon Valley line through Alloa. This magnificent ex Caledonian Railway locomotive would only be in traffic for another thirteen months.

Another delightful design of 4-4-0 this time from the North British Railway on the 26th August 1956, Class D34 62484 Glen Lyon was visiting Shore Road having worked a parcels train from Perth, where it was based. This engine would be more fortunate in surviving in work until November 1961.

Seen again in that first year of the nationalised British Railways in LNER livery was ex NBR Class C15 7469 at Shore Road on the 28th August 1948. C15 class engines worked the former LNER local passenger traffic, 7469 being a Dunfermline engine, and was another casualty of the modernising railway as she was withdrawn in 1954.

After all with so many engines to re-number and infrastructure to refresh there were a good number of ex LNER locomotives to be seen at this time such as Class J88 8351, a Stirling engine, shunting the goods sidings adjacent to Shore Road shed also on the 28th August 1948. This tank engine gained its new number 68351 in February 1951.

Among the early locomotives to gain their new identity was Class J37 64569 on the turntable at Shore Road on the 2nd November 1948. She has no smokebox numberplate and the cab numbering style follows the LNER pattern for 6 and 9. Allocated to Shore Road from the mid 1940s to 1957, 64569 was one of the last J37s to be withdrawn in December 1966.

In the 1950s Shore Road had an allocation of two ex LNER Class D49s, 62714 and 62725. On the 1st September 1956, 62714 Perthshire was present in the shed yard.   Proudly displaying the large BR emblem on its tender she was withdrawn in 1959 at a time when 4-4-0 locomotives were being displaced by newer Standard types along with ever increasing deliveries of new diesels.

Shore Road enjoyed an allocation of passenger engines for traffic to Edinburgh, either via Alloa and the Forth Bridge, or Falkirk Grahamston and Polmont. For just this type of traffic ex NBR Class D30 62426 Cuddie Headrigg would be available on the 26th May 1955. The name of this Stirling engine was drawn from the Sir Walter Scott "Waverley" series of novels, in particular Cuddie Headrigg was the ploughman in Old Mortality first published in 1816. Interestingly and by co-incidence it appears that the novel originated in a suggestion from Scott's antiquarian friend Joseph Train.

Visiting ex NBR Class J36 65237 from Fort William (shed plate 63D) along with a cab tender was captured at Shore Road on the 22nd May 1951. Like the J88 68346, a "make do and mend" approach has been applied to 65237's tender.

Bring up the Crane

At Stirling on the 19th January 1955, ex CR 3FT 56343, the "up" yard pilot, ran away near Stirling Middle signal box. For some unknown reason the engine crew had both left the footplate, leaving 56343 in reverse gear and the hand brake off. Gaining speed, 56343 ran through the "up" yard, demolished some wagons and a set of buffer stops, then embedded itself in the road banking at Forth Place. Very fortunately, no one was injured during this incident. Two days later, on Sunday the 21st January, having cleared the wagons away, the Perth steam crane and her crew were at work recovering the runaway. 56343, built in 1911 was repaired and finally withdrawn in November 1960. The unfortunate engine was stored at Cowlairs Works through that winter and cut up there early in the Spring of 1961.

Facilities for repair and maintenance of diesel locomotives at former steam sheds were initially very rudimentary. The Eastfield 45 ton steam crane was in action on the 18th September 1966 at Stirling South shed to lift one end of the Smethick built Type 2 from The Birmingham Railway Carriage and Wagon Company, in order to change a failed bogie on D5324. The bogie failure was such that the loco could not be moved, so the replacement had to be brought to the loco. The new bogie, which is shown in the foreground, together with the steam crane and four fitters from Eastfield took a full day to make the change. At this time, Stirling was officially closed to steam, though the depot was host to several diesel locomotives.

The Eastfield 45 ton steam crane hauled by a Class J37, was in action at St.Rollox shed on the 12th April 1958 to assist with repairs to the depot's turntable vacuum tractor. This activity would no doubt have interrupted the running of the shed, with locomotives being forced to work either tender first or to make alternative arrangements for turning. Without his turntable in action, the yard foreman would have to deal with engine crews most likely unhappy at the prospects of tender first running and the extra time required for turning elsewhere. The shed code for St.Rollox changed from the former LMS code of 31A in 1949 to become 65B, the British Railways code of 31A becoming Cambridge on the Eastern Region. St.Rollox would retain this engine shed coding right up until closure on the 7th November 1966, the nearby station on the route into Glasgow's Buchanan Street would close a little earlier in 1962.

Dressed for the Occasion

On the 3rd July 1961, Stirling shed was honoured to supply locomotives for a Royal Train working - three class 5MT ocomotives, two specially selected to haul the train and one would act as the standby. All were prepared in the days before the event and on 2nd July 1961 Black Fives 45396, 45214 and 45359, all allocated to Stirling, were recorded there. This is the only occasion on which a Royal Train was wholly manned and worked by Stirling based locomotives and enginemen. Stirling locomotive inspector Johnnie Morrison was in charge of the engine crews.

Locomotives Withdrawn for Scrapping

Kilmarnock works of the former G&SWR was used in the early 1950s to cut up withdrawn locomotives. On a visit there on the 10th August 1952, ex HR 4-6-0 4F, 57956 was awaiting the attention of the dismantlers. Built by Hawthorn & Leslie in 1919, and when withdrawn a few months earlier in May 1952 it had run approximately 880,000 miles in thirty three years service. When photographed, 57956 displayed the Lochgorm style of cab numerals, and was coupled to tender No.1843. The works during the 1950s and early 1960s would receive a great number of redundant Scottish locomotives for cutting up.

Class D30, 62421 Laird O'Monkbarns a St Margaret's engine, was stored serviceable for some time at Polmont shed, and was recorded there on the 22nd August 1959, adjacent to Polmont Junction signal box. Built at Cowlairs in 1914, 62421 was only officially withdrawn in June 1960 to be broken up at the works where she was built a few months later in 1960.

The scrap locomotive line at Hurlford shed on the 20th August 1959 contained five ex LMS 2Ps, and two ex CR 3F tanks. The lead 2P, 40571 was built at Derby in 1928 and would languish here for another two years until official withdrawal in August 1961.

Early LNER built D11 62671 Bailie MacWheeble an Eastfield engine, was stored serviceable at Grangemouth on the 3rd May 1958. The introduction of later LNER and BR built B1s plus the BR Standard classes ensured that little front line regular work was available for D11s from the mid 1950s onwards. Although 62671 remained at Grangemouth for some time, official withdrawal did not materialise until May 1961, some three years later.

Prince's Pier shed, at Greenock, was used to store surplus ex CR Pickersgill 4-4-0s and on the 12th September 1958, four members of that class were there, Nos 54468, 54479, 54498 and 54506. Finally withdrawn in late 1961, 54506 would remain at Prince's Pier for another three years, whilst 54468 and 54479 would be withdrawn thirteen months later, in October 1959.

Ex North British Railway Class D34, 62496 Glen Loy keeps company with dozens of other condemned locomotives at the Bo'ness dump, on the 12th May 1962, some six months after its official withdrawal. With preservation of Scottish heritage in the town today it is a great pity that the "Barry phenomenon" was not repeated in Scotland to save more locomotives for north of the border.

Grangemouth had a large allocation of ex WD engines, and on a sunny 27th April 1957 WD 2-8-0, 90199 and its bigger brother 2-10-0, 90757 were on shed, both being North British Locomotive Co. products from 1943 and 1945 respectfully and in very clean condition.

Polmont's allocation of passenger locomotives provided power for local services, including Bo'ness, and on the 6th June 1952, a very clean ex NBR C15, 67463 was simmering in the sunshine outside the shed. Directly behind 67463, which was withdrawn in a little over three years later in September 1955, are ex NBR Y9s 68104 and 68113.

Another visit to Polmont on the 28th May 1960, found one of Reid's design of short wheelbase locomotives for the North British Railway as Class J88, 68350 on her home shed basking in the sunshine. This engine and six of her class would survive into 1962, however none would remain active after that December.

The shed pilot at Motherwell on the 6th June 1953, was ex Caledonian Railway 3F 56303, resting once again in fine weather. A dual fitted engine, 56303 was built at St.Rollox in 1905 and withdrawn in August 1956 after fifty one years service. The Westinghouse brake pump is seen attached to the cab side sheeting and the air reservoir is mounted under the rear buffer beam.

Storming away from Polmont Junction after a stop is NBL built B1 61333 on an afternoon Edinburgh Waverley to Glasgow Queen Street working on 22nd August 1959. Designed for the LNER many of the class were introduced after nationalisation such as this example entering service in June 1948. It would be April 1952 when the last two went into traffic. The railway at Polmont passes very close to the Forth & Clyde Canal, which suffered a loss of revenue and decline when the railway arrived.

Far from its' spiritual home was ex GER Class J69, 68524 a Stratford product of 1905, recorded in the dead engine line at Polmont on the 9th August 1958. Two more of this class could be found based at Dundee Tay Bridge.

Grangemouth was host to a Haymarket visitor, a Gresley designed K3 mogul, 61924 on the 29th August 1959. This particular engine, was built by Armstrong Whitworth in 1934 a full ten years after the first of her class entered service for the LNER.

Another of the ex LNER Class K3 61968, a St Margaret's engine this time, was photographed during a visit to Bathgate on the 13th September 1960. Also built by Armstrong Whitworth this time in 1936. A longer term 64A based engine, once withdrawn in late 1961, she went north to Inverurie for dismantling within the works in 1962.

At Hamilton, on 6th June 1953, was a very grubby LMS built 4P, 54639 at its home shed being coaled for its next working. 54639 which was dual brake fitted, was built at St.Rollox in 1926 to the 1916 Caledonian Railway "60" class design and was the last Scottish designed 4-6-0 in regular traffic, until withdrawn in March 1954. Her frames evidence that 54639 seems to have been involved in some rough shunting!

One of the few named Class J36 locomotives 65268 Allenby was a Bathgate engine, and was also seen at its home depot on the 2nd July 1959. Built at Cowlairs in 1892, as NBR 611 this engine had served in France during the First World War, and was named after the Commander of the 3rd Army in France of 1916. The locomotives' demise from traffic came in November 1962 after seventy years of service.

In contrast to the above on the 31st May 1958, Horwich built BR Standard 4MT, 76000 was on shed at Hamilton. Built some sixty years after 65268 Allenby in 1952, she would remain a Motherwell engine thoughout her life, and when withdrawn in 1967 would be scrapped at nearby Wishaw with just fifteen years to her credit.

One of the few ex NBR Class J37s fitted for passenger stock workings with ATC was 64634, which is seen here at its home shed Bathgate, on the 16th June 1960. The ATC transducer was mounted just behind the centre of the front buffer beam, and is protected from coupling damage by a steel plate. This locomotive also benefited from fitting of carriage steam heating connections and was a product of Cowlairs in 1921.

Fife & East Scotland

A visit to Dalry Road, Edinburgh, on the 8th September 1955 found "Dunalastair IV" 54451 at its home shed. To assist photography the shed staff shunted 54451 to a favourable position using 73007, a visitor from Perth. This splendid 4-4-0 was built by the Caledonian at St.Rollox in 1913, and when photographed was coupled to tender No.6241, of 4,500 gallons capacity, built in 1921 for the Pickersgill "956" Class locomotives.

At Haymarket on the same day, ex NBR Class J83 68457, which was a steam braked only locomotive, was acting as shed pilot, whilst at St Margaret's, ex NBR J36 65305 was shunting sidings adjacent to the shed seen opposite.

Another visit to Edinburgh on the 18th September 1959 found ex LNER Class A4 60004, William Whitelaw being prepared at Haymarket for express duties alongside A3 60035 Windsor Lad. The A4 Pacific was built at Doncaster in 1937, and was running with a corridor tender.

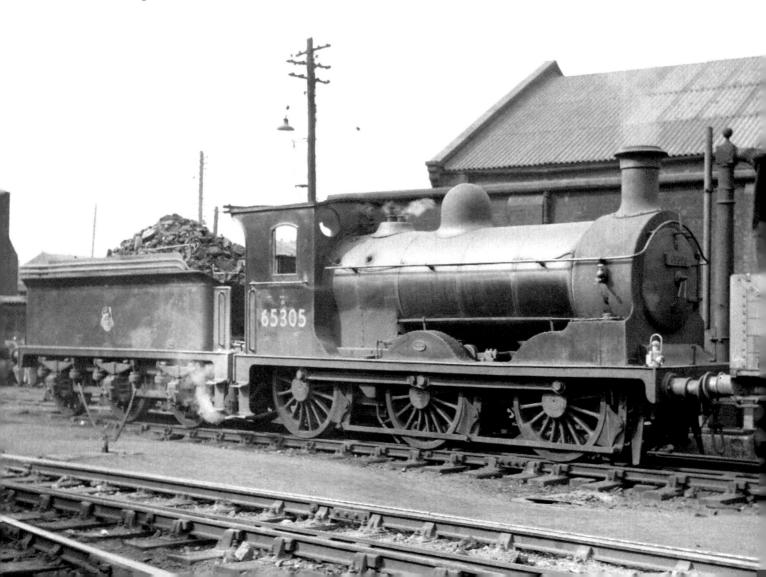

At St Margaret's on the 18th September 1959 was LMS designed 2MT 46462, at its home shed, being serviced alongside more powerful LNER designed V2 and B1 locomotives

Back to Haymarket on the same day was ex North British Railway Class N15, 69141 built by NBL in 1910 and acting as shed pilot at this busy depot.

A visit to Thornton on the 10th May 1952 found the last ex NBR Class D29 62411, Lady of Avenel inside the shed and being used as a stationary boiler. In normal circumstances shed staff would usually have obliged by shunting 62411 outside to assist photograhy. However, all that could be done was to move two J35s to give a clear shot of 62411, and attempt a time exposure. Still in LNER lined green livery, she was built at Cowlairs in 1911 and withdrawn six months later in December 1952.

Another ex NBR 4-4-0 this time a Class D30 62418, The Pirate was also captured at its home depot Thornton, seven years later on the 5th August 1959, shortly before withdrawal.

The only ex NBR Class Y9 to be vacuum fitted was 68101, a Dunfermline engine, photographed there in steam on 6th July 1957. The vacuum brake arrangements were fitted around 1937 to allow shunting of passenger stock at Dunfermline. Built in 1889, 68101 was withdrawn in November 1962 after enjoying seventy three years service.

Staying with our ex NBR theme Class D33, 62464 was in light steam at Dunfermline, its home base, on 27th June 1953. The last of her class, 62464 was built at Cowlairs in 1910 and withdrawn in September 1953, resulting in a less fruitful but still respectable forty three years of use.

The early morning sun on the 11th August 1957 catches Class J88 68346 taking water at Alloa station, whilst working the duty shunting Alloa harbour sidings. Her short wheelbase would be useful in such circumstances. There were once five stations serving this town, the first to close was Alloa Ferry in 1852, the last of the three Caledonian Railway stations, Junction, North and South would close early as well by 1885. This left all services based on the North British Railway station, which succumbed to British Railways closure in 1968.

Acting as the shed pilot on 27th June 1953 at her home shed of Dunfermline was steam braked Class N15 69192. The numbering of 69192 is consistent with the LNER layout (owner and number on tank side) and both 6 and 9 numerals accord with the LNER modification of the Gill Sans style.

The 4th August 1961 finds ex LNER Class J38 65933 trundling past Alloa shed with a westbound freight working at this once busy location.

On a visit to Greenock on the 12th September 1958, various freight locomotives were found in steam. Among the engines that day was 3F 0-6-0 57552, built in 1899 as a McIntosh "812" class. By this time 57552 was coupled to tender No.6033, of 3,570 gallons capacity, which was built in 1896, and originally provided for a McIntosh "Dunalastair I " class locomotive.

Through family connections, Hurlford shed was visited often, and on the 18th May 1957, ex LMS 2P, 40661 was resting between workings outside the rather elegant stone built shed buildings. Hurlford would gain only another four years more work from this engine before her demise.

Greenock was served by both the Glasgow & South Western Railway and the Caledonian Railways. On the 12th September 1958 a visit provides ex CR 2F, 56168, built in 1918, at Ladyburn depot, its home shed. This location would close to steam on the 26th November 1966, and completely in February 1968.

This same trip in September 1958 also took in Prince's Pier shed, where ex LMS 2F 47169 built at Derby in 1930, was busy as shed pilot and the adjacent goods yard shunter.

Back at Hurlford on the 18th May 1957 was Standard 3MT 77015, built at Swindon, and then only three years old. A wasteful twelve years service is all this engine would manage as the times were a changing.

A further visit to Hurlford on 15th April 1961 found equally short lived Standard 3MT 77019 awaiting its next duty, perhaps a local passenger turn. The shed itself would close on the last day of 1966.

When at this location on the 20th August 1959, an ex LMS 6P5F Crab 42910, built at Crewe in 1930, was preparing to leave Hurlford with the breakdown train to attend a wagons derailment at Darvel.

One of Hurlford's many ex LMS 2P 4-4-0s 40687 prepares to leave the shed for Kilmarnock on the 17th August 1958.

The following year an ex CR 3F, 57596 from Ayr, was recorded taking water at Hurlford on the 20th August 1959. This bonnie engine was built by Sharp Stewart at their Atlas Works, Glasgow in 1900 and was coupled to a 3000 gallon capacity tender, No.1768, also built in 1900.

Dropping down the coast to Stranraer we find ex CR 2F, 57445 at its home shed, on the 31st July 1956. Westinghouse braked and with its 2,800 gallon capacity tender it was built at St.Rollox in 1897, coming out of traffic finally in 1962. In the background is the former Portpatrick & Wigtown Railway works.

Inside the former G&SWR works at Kilmarnock Works on the 10th August 1952, was ex CR 4-6-2 4PT, 55361 awaiting scrapping. Built at NBL in 1917, it had spent its latter months as a Beattock banker and had been withdrawn in June 1952. To the rear of 55361 is ex HR 4-6-0 4F 57955, which had also been withdrawn in June 1952. Unfortunately 57955 could not be photographed due to limited access, and the works was on holiday, so locomotive shunting movements were not possible. Both 57956 and 55361 had travelled to Kilmarnock works under their own steam.

Barlieth Station, on the Hurlford to Darvel line, was the stop for Hurlford shed. On the 21st May 1960, home based 2P 40645 pulls away from Barlieth in charge of a Darvel to Kilmarnock local.

A view of the shed yard here on 15th April 1961 found significant steam power operating. A visitor would have found ex CR, LMS and BR Standard classes much in evidence at this time.

In front of Hurlford shed during this visit on 15th April 1961, was one of the stalwarts of the Ayrshire coalfield in ex LMS Crab 42744. With just over another year to go before she would become one of the thirty of her class to be scrapped at McWilliams yard at Shettleston in Glasgow, in the race to dispense with steam.

Stirling - Burghmuir (from 1949 Stirling South)

Burghmuir shed, half a mile south of Stirling Station, supplied motive power for a variety of traffic, including the Oban line, passenger services to Edinburgh and Glasgow, together with local industrial and colliery traffic. The shed was built for the Scottish Central Railway in the 1850s and remained in its original four road form throughout its life, save for the removal of the south gable wall in 1952, when the gable was deemed unsafe.

The largest powered locomotives allocated to Burghmuir were Stanier 5MTs, though by virtue of its position on the LMS main line to the north, the depot was often host to failures, and a large variety of motive power, from the most to the least powerful could be found there. Stirling also had the advantage of being a stop-over point for locomotives travelling under their own steam to various works for repair or breaking-up.

A view of Stirling South from the coaling stage on 14th July 1956, showing the north end of the shed. The locomotives shown are typical of what was to be found there on a normal working day: ex CR 2F and 3F engines, LMS 4Fs, a WD 2-8-0 and the ever present Stanier 5MTs.

A rather majestic LMS built 4P 14646 was on the turntable at Burghmuir on the 13th November 1948. These locomotives were regular visitors to Stirling. Allocated the British Railways number 54646 she was withdrawn as 14646 in August 1949. At this time she was allocated a 28A shed plate which was Motherwell.

Quite remarkably, Class Y9 8103 was captured at Stirling South on the 27th June 1954. It had retained its LNER number and livery some six years post nationalisation. 8103 had no shedplate or smokebox numberplate, though Dundee was stencilled on the front buffer beam. The little engine was travelling under its own steam from Dundee to Cowlairs, where it was scrapped in July 1954.

Typical of engines still used for local passenger turns in the early/middle 1950s is dual fitted ex CR 2F 57339, a Stirling engine. Built at St.Rollox in 1892 and when seen on 14th August 1956, was running coupled to tender No.1472, a 3,000 gallon variety, also built at St.Rollox but in 1918. The locomotive was withdrawn in 1959 after sixty seven years service.

The station pilot at Stirling for many years was Lambie designed 0-4-4 tank 15122, which was present at Burghmuir on the 15th April 1950. Built at St.Rollox in 1895, and originally fitted with condensing apparatus for working in the underground sections of Caledonian lines in Glasgow, the condensing equipment was removed from 1917 onwards. This old favourite was withdrawn in January 1952, having suffered a cracked main cylinder block, due to being started with the cylinder drain cocks closed.

Heading for Edinburgh and passing Stirling South sheds with a service from Stirling is ex LMS 4MT 42268 on the 2nd June 1953. After a spell at 64C Dalry Road this engine passed to 66A Polmadie for just over four years, before spending a year on the dump at Lugton. Four months stored at 66B Motherwell followed, before a swift cutting up at the yard of Messers Wards at Langloan in March 1964.

Whilst ex NBR Class C15 tank engines would not normally be associated with the LMS shed at Stirling, 67454 was to be found there on the 4th January 1953. It had been transferred to Stirling in December 1952 from Eastfield (the loco carried a 65C, Parkhead, shedplate) for trials on the Devon Valley line, but apparently proved unsuitable, since 67454 was returned to Eastfield in February 1953, and was withdrawn in June 1954. Of additional interest in the photograph is the wooden Caledonian Railway plough attached to the 2F directly behind the C15.

Local coal traffic from Manor Powis colliery was shared with locomotives based at Stirling and Alloa. Dunfermline allocated Class J36 65323, complete with cab tender was captured at Stirling on the 11th January 1958 for just such a turn.

On the 16th December 1955, Stanier designed ex LMS 5MT 44701 is seen storming past Stirling South sheds with the "Up" Saint Mungo - Aberdeen to Glasgow Buchanan Street express.

Through the kindness of a telephone message from George Maxwell, the Stirling South shedmaster, the preserved ex GNSR No 49, Gordon Highlander was recorded in steam at Stirling on the 10th June 1959. The graceful 4-4-0's trip to Stirling was part of a running-in schedule after the locomotive had been given a major repair, and prior to its use on special trains. As with Ben Alder seen below, No 49 had developed a hot tender axlebox and repairs were carried out at Stirling.

Once again via a telephone call from the shed foreman to the family home, advising that an unusual locomotive had arrived at Stirling South, my father recorded 54398, Ben Alder there on the 8th November 1958. The "Small Ben" had been towed from Perth that day by a 5MT, but had run hot at Dunblane and it was decided to stop at Stirling to affect repairs. 54398's coupling rods were stowed in the tender, and the boiler backhead carried a brass plate denoting the boiler as "Class 34 - 2270". Whilst 54398 was built at Dubs & Co in 1898, when photographed at Stirling, the locomotive was coupled to tender No.1800, a 3,000 gallon variety, built in 1899. On 8th November 1958 this venerable engine was being moved to St.Rollox for storage, with the intention of preservation, which tragically did not take place.

Even as late as 1957, work could be found for ex CR 4-4-0 locomotives. 54485, allocated to Stirling, is seen at the sheds on the 2nd November 1957, being prepared for piloting a southbound express to Carlisle. The express, which left Perth headed by a Stanier 5MT, should have been provided with class 6 power, but none was available. Perth shed had telephoned to Stirling to provide a second 5MT as pilot, but the only available loco at Stirling was 54485. The Perth driver's words were unprintable when 54485 backed on to his train as pilot - a case of take it or leave it. Anyway, 54485 left Stirling and successfully piloted to Carstairs where a further 5MT was attached.

Built by Neilson & Co. in 1899 for the Caledonian Railway and now classified as a 3F, 57576 was coupled to tender No.1765, a 3,000 gallon variety built in 1919 when seen with her cheerful crew at Stirling on the 28th March 1959. This happy scene would only last for another couple of years as the locomotive was withdrawn in September 1961.

Oban based ex CR 2P 55196, carrying a 63E shedplate, and sporting a capped chimney, was recorded at the shed on the 21st August 1953. Displaying the full set of front-end hose connections: from the left they are vacuum brake, Westinghouse brake and carriage heating. By this time the south gable of the shed had been removed.

DANGER
←—→
LIMITED
CLEARANCE

55196

63
E

On the 8th April 1957, ex CR 3F 56375 was the shed pilot at Stirling South. Built at St.Rollox in 1922 she was a steam braked only locomotive. At some repair period a short chimney had been substituted for her original. This replacement chimney is too short to have come from a CR "812" class engine, and seems to be of the type originally fitted to CR eight-coupled "492" class tank engines. In the August of the following year she would be withdrawn and sent to Kilmarnock Works for disposal like many of her kin.

On the 26th May 1956, Stirling South shed was required to provide a standby engine for a Royal Train working. The best of the local 5MTs, 45214, was selected for this duty and is shown at the shed in standby condition, with white painted buffers and shedplate. The chargehand fitter responsible for preparing 45214 mechanically, Sandy Paris, is second from the left in this group.

A longer term Perth based Black Five 45171 from one of the Armstong Whitworth batches shows off the tablet apparatus along with the riveted style of tender on the 29th October 1954. Many of the routes these engines would have ventured over would be single track. This locomotive when built would have had a domeless boiler.

Although of poorer quality, this shot, taken at Stirling on a rainy 18th August 1951, of the original CR No. 60, now numbered 54650 by BR, has been included since it shows 54650 to have been given the early BR livery. Some authorities suggest that 14560, was withdrawn in September 1953 without carrying a BR livery. This engine was built at St.Rollox in 1916 and was based at Motherwell in 1951.

One of Gresley's fine V2 locomotives, 60955 from Aberdeen Ferryhill was recorded on the Stirling South turntable on the 15th June 1957. Built at Darlington in 1942 and was now coupled to tender No. 4790, built at Darlington in 1937. At a time of severe motive power shortage, Stirling shed sent a V2 on the Oban route, where they were not permitted to operate. The V2 in question got as far as Callander, until it fouled the platform edge.

Jubilee class locomotives were very familiar on through expresses - here on 2nd May 1959, is Perth based 6P 45727, Inflexible which was built at Crewe and released to traffic on the 12th October 1936. On this day it was gracing the shed yard at Stirling but it would one of twenty three Jubilees to be withdrawn en masse in October 1962. On the right is home based 5MT 45214 also awaiting her next turn.

The last known operational steam locomotive to be serviced at Stirling, a month after the shed officially closed to steam was 2-8-0 WD Austerity 90370, which suffered a big end failure at Stirling on the 9th July 1966. Allocated to Wakefield at this time, 90370 would find itself breaking the long association with the Yorkshire shed to see out her last ten months of service based at Sunderland. One of the North British Locomotive Co. batches built in September 1944 for War Department Ministry of Supply use, this engine first went to Belgium, based at Ostend, before her return to Great Britain.

British Railways Crewe Works turned out Class 6MT 72000 Clan Buchanan in 1951. She was still a comparative youngster when as a Polmadie based engine my father recorded her at Stirling on the 9th May 1959, after working a Mossend to Stirling freight. It was rare for my father to photograph newer locomotives as his passion was for pre-grouping types with obscure detail differences, but we are grateful for this exception as this particular Clan had only three more years of active duty before being withdrawn in 1962.

On the 17th August 1965, with all of the pre-grouping types gone, Britannia 7P 70008 was photographed at Stirling. Named Black Prince 70008 was devoid of nameplates and locomotive builder' plates: the tender coupled was BR1 No.767 with 4,250 gallons capacity, built in 1951. This once magnificent prince was a Carlisle Kingmoor engine at this time.

Having been coaled to take over as station pilot, ex CR 2P 55176 was ready for duty when seen at Stirling South shed on the 5th November 1955. Not enhanced by its stove-pipe chimney, 55176 was a Stirling engine for many years, being a product of St.Rollox in 1910 and withdrawn in November 1958 to be quickly cut up by the Kilmarnock Works fitters the following month.

Throughout the winter months, Stirling South shed kept a snow-plough engine in steam and on twenty four hour constant standby to deal with regular heavy snowfalls on the Oban line. If conditions demanded, two 4Fs would be coupled together. On the 29th December 1956, ex Midland Railway 4F, 43884 was allocated to this duty and is shown coupled to a new medium steel plough, which had replaced the ex CR wooden ploughs in 1954. Having been built at Derby in 1919, this engine would go on to serve at both Polmadie and Motherwell, before being broken up staying north of the border at Connells yard at Calder in June 1962.

On the night of 19th January 1957, Class N2 69503 passed through Stirling under its own steam en-route to Cowlairs for scrapping. The running foreman at the shed telephoned the family home and this flashlight photograph was the result. Previously 69503 had been allocated to Aberdeen Ferryhill, and was built for the Great Northern Railway in 1921.

One of the last ex CR 2F 0-6-0s to survive at Stirling was 57261, a steam braked only machine, seen here on the 23rd March 1961, carrying a 65J shedplate. 57261 having rolled out of the Caledonian Railway's works at St.Rollox in 1884 would soldier on until withdrawn in December 1963, enjoying a working life of seventy nine years. The tender coupled to 57261 was No.1672 of 3,000 gallons capacity, built in 1900.

On 9th May 1959, en-route to St.Rollox for overhaul was ex LMS 3P 40011 stopped over at Stirling. Allocated to Keith at the time, 40011 was built at Derby in 1930.

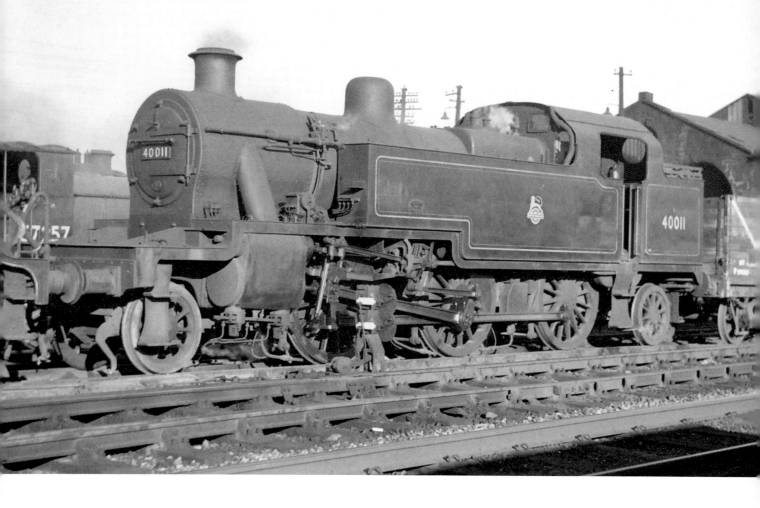

Perth based Jubilee class 6P, 45677 Beatty was also a visitor to Stirling on the 11th May 1960. A product of the LMS at Crewe in 1935, at this time was coupled to a Type 1 tender No.10504, of 4,000 gallons capacity, built in 1945.

Another of the Armstrong Whitworth built Black Fives 45127 charges past Stirling South sheds with an Oban to Glasgow Buchanan Street working on the 12th June 1962.

An unusual visitor to Stirling on the 8th July 1960 was London based Patriot class 45547, at the time coupled to a Fowler 3,500 gallon tender. The locomotive had arrived heading a fitted freight from Carlisle.

An unwelcome stranger to Stirling on the 21st March 1959 was Metropolitan Vickers Co-Bo D5711, which had come north with a freight from Mossend. This box like diesel is shown approaching Stirling Station, framed by the signal gantry spanning the four parallel running lines which ran from the station to Stirling South signal box.

A far more elegant and impressive piece of machinery to arrive at the shed on 25th September 1965 was A4 60024 Kingfisher which had been stopped for repairs. This locomotive was to escape work on the Glasgow to Aberdeen runs for railtours to the Dorset coast and to Exeter in 1966.

Stirling South was occasional host to other glamour engines in the shape of ex LMS 8P 46236 City of Bradford on the 22nd May 1963.

Perhaps the more typical image of the shed in its latter years was of Black Five 5MT 45084 at Stirling on the 16th October 1965

North East, Perth, Aberdeen, Dundee and the Oban Line

At Perth on the 3rd September 1962, Standard Class 5MT 73107, which was a Perth regular had arrived at Eastfield shed from Doncaster Works in December 1955. After nine years of service a move to Grangemouth followed in December 1964. Two further moves would take her to Stirling in October 1965 and finally back to Glasgow to spend the last three months out of Corkerhill when withdrawn in September 1966 after just eleven years service. That said the Scottish allocated Standard Fives put in higher annual average mileages than their counterparts on other regions.

Acting as Forfar shed pilot on the 29th July 1958 was ex CR 3F 56290, emerging from St.Rollox in 1905. She was ideal for such shed and station pilot work being a Westinghouse braked engine, with vacuum ejector for working vacuum braked stock, but was withdrawn eleven months after this visit.

At Perth on the 14th September 1956 both ex NBR and ex CR 4-4-0s were to be found working. Ex CR 3P, 54503 a Perth based engine, also built at St.Rollox this time in 1922, was active as shed pilot. Behind 54503 with a bent buffer beam, is stored LMS 4P compound 40939.

Approaching Glen Ogle summit, and steaming hard, on the 6th July 1955, named 5MT 45154, The Lanarkshire Yeomanry has command of the 1.09pm Stirling to Oban passenger working.

One of the British Railways built but LMS designed 2MT moguls 46468 was at Oban on 1st July 1961. Often employed on the Ballachulish goods workings she was built at Darlington in 1951 and carries the perhaps less visually appealing narrow chimney which is not improved by the small piece knocked out.

A popular location to visit for many photographers from the era, with my father being no exception was Killin Pier shed. This visit on the 6th July 1955, rewards us with ex CR 2P 55126, originally fitted with condensing apparatus when built at St.Rollox in 1897 and filling out her last years before the arrival of the Standard tanks and her despatch to the scrapmen in 1961.

On the 12th June 1954, Black Five 45474 was recorded passing through C&O Junction, Dunblane, heading an Oban to Stirling freight working. The view was taken from C&O Junction signal box with the kindness of the signalman.

Stanier 5MT 44970 at Balquidder East, on the 6th July 1955, heading the 9.18am Oban to Glasgow, Buchanan Street, with through carriages to Edinburgh Princes Street.

At Perth on the 14th September 1956 ex NBR Class D34 62470, Glen Roy a Perth engine, built at Cowlairs in 1913, was about to leave the shed on a Devon Valley goods working.

Perth again six years later on the 3rd September 1962 and Class A3 60037 Hyperion a visitor from St Margaret's, was being serviced on the shed. Carrying smoke deflectors, double chimney and a banjo dome perhaps improves the appearance of these engines from their original as built condition. These modifications certainly helped this thoroughbred through a respectable twenty nine years service.

On the 22nd June 1957, Z4 68190 was found in light steam within Kittybrewster shed.

A very wet 8th July 1950, and ex GNSR D40 62261 was at Aberdeen, Kittybrewester. She was built by Neilson Reid & Co in 1899 and withdrawn in March 1953. When photographed, the loco had no smokebox numberplate and the cab numbers were painted using the LNER style of 6.

Fellow ex GNSR tank engine from Class Z5 on this same visit has gained her 68193 smokebox numberplate. Both types of tank engines were built by Manning Wardle in 1915 for use on the Aberdeen harbour branch, and the photographs show that both retain their original spring balance safety valves with easing lever extended into the respective cabs.

On the same wet day, ex GNSR Z4 tank engine 68191 was captured at the Kittybrewster coaling stage in similar livery.

These same poor weather conditions, forced my father into this view of another GNSR survivor Class D41 62225 also at Kittybrewster on 8th July 1950. Like the D40 opposite she was slightly older and built by Neilson & Co in 1893 and withdrawn in 1953 after sixty faithful years service.

The very grimy St.Combs branch engine, Standard 2MT 78053 a more modern design from Darlington in 1955, was on parade at the Granite City's other shed at Ferryhill on the 26th September 1961. This scruffy little mogul was withdrawn in 1964 after only nine years service.

Also taken at Ferryhill was this view of ex NBR Class N15, 69128, on the 22nd June 1958. A Westinghouse braked engine, 69128 was built by NBL in Glasgow in 1910.

Inside Arbroath shed on the evening of 31st August 1958, and Class C16 67502 was parked within the shed and all staff were off duty, so only an internal shot was available.   At this time the three road shed housed six stored engines (four D11s, one J36 and one J72), 67502 was the only engine in steam.

A visit to the town a week previously and 2MT 46463 was attending as the station pilot at Arbroath on the 23rd July 1958 whilst shunting the adjacent goods sidings.

Visiting Dundee West on the 14th September 1956, provides ex NBR Class D30, 62438 Peter Poundtext having returned to the shed from a ballast train working. Unusually, 62438 was carrying a boiler using lock-up safety valves, which may have come from a withdrawn D32.

Two further veterans such as Y9 68108 and J36 65319 could be found at Dundee Tay Bridge shed on the same day in 1956.

Glasgow Area

Resting between duties at Eastfield on an inclement 15th September 1958 was ex NBR Class C15 67460. Fitted with push-pull equipment for working the Tarbet to Arrochar line, the layout of Westinghouse brake pump and push-pull apparatus is clearly seen.

Always kept in fine fettle was the St.Rollox Works shunting engine 56025, as on the 26th August 1953. Classified by British Railways as 0F these little "Pugs" had been introduced by the Caledonian Railway for shunting the many dockyard lines they served.

In a visit together we recorded at Cowlairs Works ex NBR Class J83 68467, a Thornton engine, on the 29th September 1954.

"Dunalastair IV" 54458, an Inverness engine, was a fine sight at St.Rollox shed on 21st August 1954. Built in 1916, 54458 was being run-in after works overhaul and was withdrawn in 1958. When photographed, 54458 was coupled to tender No.6177, of 4,200 gallons capacity, also built in 1916.

On September the 15th 1955, ex CR 3F 57557, a St.Rollox engine, was at its home shed in light steam. A Westinghouse braked engine, she was coupled to tender No. 6031, of 3,570 gallon capacity, built in 1896, which had originally been attached to a "Dunalastair I" Class 4-4-0.

On the 4th February 1950, ex HR 4-6-0 54767 Clan Mackinnon was stopped at St.Rollox shed en-route from Inverness to Kilmarnock for breaking up. The then shed master at St.Rollox, Mr John Brown, stands before 54767, which was built by Hawthorn Leslie in 1921.

British Railways continued with this distinctive naming tradition with 6MT 72007, Clan MacIntosh seen here at Corkerhill on the 15th September 1959. This particular Clan lasted fifteen years less than the one above.

Dawsholm was home to a number of ex LMS 3P locomotives such as 40189 here on 26th August 1960.

In the early 1960s ex NBR 4-4-0s could still be found at work in Scotland, as evidenced by D34 62496, Glen Loy in steam at its home depot, Eastfield, on the 26th August 1960. Built in 1920, this "Glen" was withdrawn in late 1961.

Another Dawsholm engine ex CR 2F 56169, still in original BR livery, was at St.Rollox on the 14th July 1951. She had been built at the works here in 1900.

Ex NBR Class J83 8479 was acting as Eastfield shed pilot when a visit was made on the 16th August 1949. To assist with rolling stock movements and banking from Queen Street station 8479 she was fitted with a slip coupling.

On the 7th July 1951, Class N14 69120 was decorated in early BR livery at Eastfield. A Westinghouse fitted engine, she was one of a small class built in 1909 for Cowlairs incline banking duties: a slip coupling pulley was fitted to the right hand smokebox front.   The last of her class 69120 was withdrawn in 1954.

The preserved ex Caledonian Railway No. 123 was kept at Dawsholm, along with ex Great North of Scotland Railway No.49, during a visit on 15th September 1959. The pair were being prepared for a special train working.

Designed with a completely different objective was Sir William Stanier's 8F 48708, this one being built during the war in 1944 by the Southern Railway. Now in peacetime and allocated to Carlisle Kingmoor, she had come north to Polmadie on the 26th September 1963.

At a time when diesels outnumbered steam on the 14th August 1965, BR Standard Class 4MT 80120 waits its next turn of duty at Polmadie. Also built in the south at Brighton in 1955 this locomotive would hang on here until that last trip to Campbells scrapyard at Airdrie in 1967.

Steam was everywhere on the 16th August 1949, when my father was rewarded with a shot of N15 69198 in the early British railways livery, before the application of a smokebox numberplate and still favouring the LNER style of numbers for 6 and 9 on the bunker sides.

In the late 1940s ex HR 3F 0-6-0s were allocated to Corkerhill and two of these survivors were still here on the 4th February 1950. Wearing 17694 in LMS livery she would survive for a further two years.

A true Highland survivor was 4-6-0 No.103, withdrawn by the LMS as 17916 in 1934, and kept at St.Rollox works, where it was sought out on the 26th August 1953. At this time 103 was in an "as withdrawn" state, having a tablet exchanger bolted to the left hand cab side and being devoid of smokebox wingplates.

Unlike 17694 above photographed on the same day at Corkerhill, classmate 57698 had already had the earliest British Railways livery applied. Both locomotives were purchased from Dubs & Co in 1900 by the Highland Railway.

Men and Machines

At Beattock shed on the 9th August 1949, ex Caledonian Railway Class "944" now as BR 4PT, 55360 carrying a 12F shedplate and dressed in the initial BR livery, was being prepared for further banking workings by its crew. Through the local Motive Power Superintendent, my father had two return trips to Beattock summit on 55360, whilst banking northbound trains. Built by NBL in 1917, 55360 was withdrawn in February 1952.

Burghmuir shed at Stirling was host to ex CR 2F 57334 and her crew on the 2nd September 1950. Based at Grangemouth and in early style BR livery, this engine was one of the very few 2Fs to retain the original Drummond brake gear, in which the brake hangers are coupled by rodding external to the wheel rims. Built at St.Rollox in 1892, 57334 was set aside for scrap in March 1951.

Stirling South dealt with the servicing of many additional locomotives for the working of twenty two special trains, related to a Bannockburn rally, on the 28th May 1960. All available shed space was pressed into service, and at a relatively quiet moment, some of the crews with their locos posed for the photographer. The specials were worked by LNER B1s, LMS 5MTs and BR 5MTs.

John Birkhill, the Stirling South running foreman, poses with his "new toy", D2742 on 2nd May 1959. This wonder of the modern world was delivered new from NBL some weeks previously, but by July 1964 she had no work to perform at Stirling. After a transfer first to Eastfield this unfortunate locomotive would be passed on to Crewe Works to act as a works shunter until February 1967. Out of favour as diesel locomotive manufacturers this North British Locomotive Company product was sold to scrap men at Ickles.

On the 22nd August 1958, Hurlford shedmaster William Macrae stands with D3009, which had been acquired by Hurlford some years earlier. The location is Barlieth mineral sidings adjacent to Hurlford depot. My father had a go at driving this diesel, which greatly simplified the shunting process and which was much welcomed by enginemen. The author peers from the cab.

In October 1959 the track layout at the south end of Stirling shed was completely renewed. This manpower intensive operation was carried out over a weekend and the permanent way gangers were recorded at work.

Driver Ferguson stands with his locomotive an ex LMS 4F, 44320 at Grangemouth, the engine's home shed on the 21st June 1958. This Scottish 4F would hang on at 65F until October 1962, then withdrawn she would stay at her home depot until final cutting up at Motherwell Machinery & Scrap Company at Wishaw in September 1963, thirty six years after her construction at St.Rollox in 1927.

It was on the 11th June 1966, that Stirling South shed officially closed to steam power working after approximately one hundred and twenty years service. The last working steam locomotive to leave the shed on that day was a very dirty and unkempt BR 5MT 73154, which carried a 65J shedplate, with St.Rollox stencilled on the front buffer beam. This unique event was captured with the engine's crew: driver Peter Scott and fireman James Maillie, the two running foreman along with George Maxwell, the shedmaster, wearing a trilby hat. Built at Derby in 1956, Caprotti fitted 73154 coupled to a BR1B tender of 4,725 gallons capacity, was withdrawn later in December 1966 after only ten years in service.

Mishaps and Machines

At Grangemouth West Yard, on the 17th August 1959, the crew of one of the Riddles Austerity designed 2-10-0 locomotives 90759, were recorded together with the members of the re-railing gang and John Anderson, the Grangemouth shedmaster, in the hat, while attempting to get this Grangemouth allocated WD's tender back on the rails. Notoriously rough riders, this WD's tender had become derailed at a set of points. After burning through the projecting tender buffers, 90759's tender was jacked back on to the track and the crew set off, light engine, for Grangemouth shed. My father drove 90759 some three miles to the depot, with the driver acting as pilotman.

Whilst visiting Thornton shed on the 10th May 1952, an engine movement resulted in ex LNER D49, 62729 Rutlandshire running into the side of ex NBR J35 64522. Damage was slight, though there was much embarrassment to shed staff as the photographer, displaying his region-wide shed pass, recorded the event.

Having been involved in a major "head-on" incident at Maryhill in early September 1963, English Electric Type 1 D8073 was awaiting repairs at Dawsholm on the 11th of that month. The diesel had been in service for just twenty six months at that time, after repairs it would serve another twenty eight years.

A Select Bibliography

A Detailed History of British Railways Standard Steam Locomotives Volume Two: The 4-6-0 and 2-6-0 Classes.
RCTS 2003.

Scottish Steam in the 1950s and '60s.
David Anderson, OPC 1997.

British Railways Steam Locomotives 1948-1968.
Hugh Longworth, OPC 2005.

Gresley Locomotives A Pictorial History.
Brian Haresnape, Ian Allan 1981.

BR Steam Motive Power Depots Scr.
Paul Bolger, Ian Allan 1983.

The Book of the Jubilee 4-6-0s.
Chris Hawkins, Irwell Press 2002.

Diesel & Electric Locomotive Register.
Alan Sugden, Platform 5 1994.

The Allocation History of B.R. Diesels and Electrics.
Roger Harris, 1985.

Complete British Railways Maps and Gazeteer 1825-1985.
C.J. Wignall, OPC 1983.

What Happened to Steam.
P.B. Hands

Reference has also been made to various issues of the following journals; Railway Observer, Railway Magazine, Railway World, Trains Illustrated, Modern Railways.

Reference has also been made to the notebooks of the Late Alexander Ian Peddie.

Abbreviations used in this book

ATC	Automatic Train Control
BR	British Railways
	British Rail (from 1.1965)
C&O	Callander & Oban Railway
CR	Caledonian Railway
GER	Great Eastern Railway
GNSR	Great North of Scotland Railway
G&SWR	Glasgow & South Western Railway
HR	Highland Railway
LMS	London Midland & Scottish Railway
LNER	London & North Eastern Railway
NBL	North British Locomotive Company
NBR	North British Railway
WD	War Department

Help To Preserve Our Railway Heritage

In addition to publishing books on our Railway Heritage Strathwood have also set up a Charitable Trust to house an archive of images comprising over 200,000 photographic negatives and slides.

The archive was established to not only preserve the collections of over one hundred photographers both living and deceased, but to also make their work available to a younger audience for the future. To achieve this aim, we have begun an energetic programme to publish a considerable number of books. Allied to this we are making as many as possible of the photographs and slides we hold, available as copies to interested enthusiasts, individuals, societies and other publishers.

Many photographers have chosen Strathwood to care for their collections and to publish the best examples of their work for posterity.

If you have negatives or colour slides of transport subjects then we would like to hear from you. We purchase, accept on loan, or welcome donations of material to the archive. Photographers always receive recognition for their work when it is used by publishers (A N Other/Strathwood Library).

Please make contact now if you would like to see your work in print, perhaps in a similar fashion to this publication. We also undertake publications to benefit charities and societies on behalf of our contributors. In addition we can store, and catalogue collections on behalf of clubs and societies by way of loan, thereby releasing such groups to concentrate on other aspects of their activities.

Strathwood Ltd,
Glenavon House,
Kinchurdy Road,
Boat of Garten,
Inverness-shire,
PH24 3BP.

Telephone 01479 831139

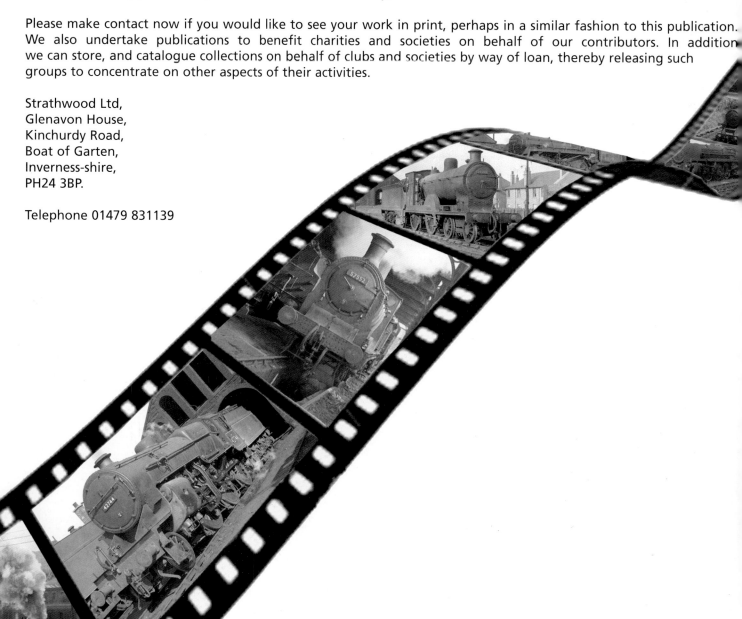